Young Learner

QUICK, SMART

PUNCTUATION

Developed by

Neeti Kaushik
Post Graduate (Education)
(Active in the field of education
for the past 14 years)

Anamika Dutta
Post Graduate (English Literature)

Neeti and Anamika are involved in developing creative and interactive reading material for children. They have also authored books on Environment, Life Skills and Preschool Concepts.

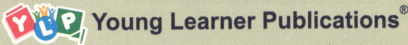
Young Learner Publications®

Index

GRAMMAR SCRAPBOOK: ‹ ••••

Punch and tag a few sheets of art paper into a booklet. Use old greeting cards to make the cover.

RESOURCES: ‹ ••••

Use pictures from old books, magazines, newspapers, posters and greeting cards. Check out some smart ideas given in the book!

Printed at : SRG Traders Pvt. Ltd., B-41, Sec-67, Noida

© Young Learner Publications

Understanding

Punctuation is used to bring clarity and meaning to writing.

Let us see why punctuation is an important element of grammar. Read this funny story about a man who really loved bread. The story is without punctuation!

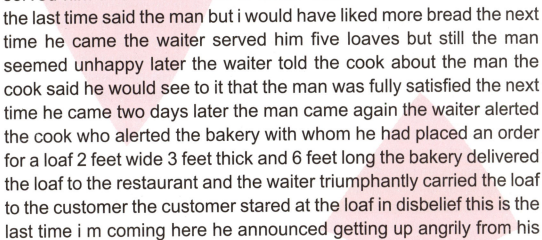

a man eating in a restaurant called the waiter and complained that he had been given only one loaf with his meat dish i like lots of bread said the man remember that next time the next time he came the waiter served him three loaves this is better than the last time said the man but i would have liked more bread the next time he came the waiter served him five loaves but still the man seemed unhappy later the waiter told the cook about the man the cook said he would see to it that the man was fully satisfied the next time he came two days later the man came again the waiter alerted the cook who alerted the bakery with whom he had placed an order for a loaf 2 feet wide 3 feet thick and 6 feet long the bakery delivered the loaf to the restaurant and the waiter triumphantly carried the loaf to the customer the customer stared at the loaf in disbelief this is the last time i m coming here he announced getting up angrily from his

chair and throwing his napkin on the table i keep telling you i want more bread and here you are once again serving me just one loaf

Did you find it difficult to understand the story?   YES☐   NO☐

Now, let us read the same story after punctuating it.

A man eating in a restaurant called the waiter and complained that he had been given only one loaf with his meat dish. "I like lots of bread," said the man. "Remember that next time."

The next time he came the waiter served him three loaves. "This is better than the last time," said the man. "But I would have liked more bread."

The next time he came the waiter served him five loaves but still the man seemed unhappy. Later the waiter told the cook about the man. The cook said he would see to it that the man was fully satisfied the next time he came.

Two days later the man came again. The waiter alerted the cook who alerted the bakery with whom he had placed an order for a loaf 2 feet wide, 3 feet thick and 6 feet long. The bakery delivered the loaf to the restaurant, and the waiter triumphantly carried the loaf to the customer. The customer stared at the loaf in disbelief. "This is the last time I'm coming here!" he announced getting up angrily from his chair and throwing his napkin on the table. "I keep telling you I want more bread and here you are once again serving me just one loaf!"

Did you find it easy to understand the story this time?
YES ☐ **NO** ☐

Use of Capital Letters

Understanding

> A capital letter is used at the beginning of a sentence.

Examples

The bear in the zoo was a big one.

Cycling is a good form of exercise.

His favourite pastime is reading mystery stories.

Understanding

> A capital letter is used with proper nouns.

Examples

On Saturday morning, we have an Inter School Soccer Match.

Roger is a good tennis player.

Mother Teresa was born in Skopje, Macedonia, on Monday, August 27, 1910.

Examples

A capital letter is used with adjectives that are derived from proper nouns.

1. David Copperfield is my favourite Dickensian character.
2. We had dinner at a Chinese restaurant.
3. Most tombs of the Mughal era were inspired by Persian architecture.

Understanding

The pronoun "I" is always written in capital.

Example

My parents say I spend too much time surfing the net. I think it's a great way to gather information.

Understanding

In titles, the first letter of each main word is capitalized.

Examples

1. Buckingham Palace is the home to the Queen of England.
2. He has a degree in Nuclear Physics from the Cambridge University.

PRACTICE

A. Fill in the missing capital letters.

Proper Nouns	Adjectives
India	__ ndian
Europe	__ uropean
France	__ rench
New York	__ ew __ orker
China	__ hinese
Malaysia	__ alaysian

B. Circle the letters that should be capitalized in the given paragraph.

today, me and my friend ted drove to the manchester club. the pine trees that lined up along the main road looked beautiful! we passed through the river bridge. then we drove across the tom square palace. the guards outside the palace did not let us in.

3

Punctuation marks are symbols that help us to organize and structure sentences. The term punctuation is derived from a Latin term *punctum*. It means the correct use of points or stops in writing.

The chart below lists some punctuation marks and a few rules.

Punctuation marks	Uses	Examples
A	**Capital letter:** 1. starts a sentence 2. indicates proper nouns 3. emphasizes certain words	All I want is a pastry. You can call me Ronnie. I want it TODAY!
.	**Full stop:** ends sentences that are not questions or exclamations	This is a sentence.
?	**Question mark:** ends sentences that are questions	Is this your assignment?
!	**Exclamation mark:** ends a sentence that is an exclamation	Don't pick that!
" "	**Quotation (speech) marks:** enclose direct speech (can be double or single)	"Help me!" the man yelled.
,	**Comma:** 1. places a pause between clauses within a sentence 2. separates items in a list 3. separates adjectives in a series	We were late, although it didn't matter. You will need eggs, butter, salt and cheese. I wore a red-coloured, long and frilly skirt.

Punctuation marks	Uses	Examples
,	4. completely encloses clauses inserted in a sentence 5. marks speech from words denoting who said them	We were, though we had rushed to get there, late for the film. 'Thank you,' I said.
-	**Hyphen:** connects elements of certain words	Co-ordinator, north-east.
:	**Colon:** 1. introduces lists (including examples) 2. introduces summaries 3. introduces (direct) quotations 4. introduces a second clause that expands or illustrates the meaning of the first	We learned the following at the camp: rock climbing, canoeing and rafting. During the salsa class we were told: dance salsa on any beat or across the beat. My instructor always says: "bend those knees." The snow hardened: it turned into ice.
;	**Semicolon:** 1. separates two closely linked clauses and shows that there is a link between them 2. separates items in a complex list	On Tuesday, the tram was late; the bus was early. You can go by an aeroplane, train and a taxi; channel tunnel train, coach, then a short walk; or aeroplane and car.
'	**Apostrophe of possession:** denotes the ownership of something	This is Betsy's scarf. These are Peter's books.
'	**Apostrophe of contraction:** shows the omission of a letter(s) when two (or occasionally more) words are contracted	Don't walk on the grass. She'd've told us. (double contraction is used in spoken English only)

Punctuation marks	Uses	Examples
	**Ellipsis:** 1. shows the omission of words 2. indicates a pause	The teacher moaned, "Look at this floor... a mess... this class." Louis said: 'I think I locked the door... no, hang on ... did I ?'
	**Brackets:** set apart a word or phrase added to a sentence to give some additional information	The necklace (which had been in my family for years) was stolen.
	**Dash:** 1. indicates additional information, with more emphasis than a comma 2. indicates a pause, especially for effect at the end of a sentence 3. contains extra information (used instead of brackets)	She is an author – and a very good one too. We all know what to expect – the best. You solved that sum – and I don't know how – before anybody else.

FOR YOUR GRAMMAR SCRAPBOOK

Make a similar chart in your scrapbook using all the punctuation signs.

Understanding

A full stop marks the end of a sentence. While reading a sentence we need to pause after a full stop.

Examples

A full stop is used at the end of every telling sentence.

1. An elephant has a long trunk.

2. Mr James is an excellent teacher.

3. India is a fascinating country.

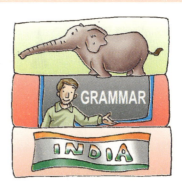

Understanding

A full stop is used at the end of an abbreviated word or between the letters of an abbreviated word.

Examples

Co. (company)   a.m. (short for Latin *ante meridiem*)

Dept. (department)   e.g. (for example)

i.e. (short for Latin *id est*, meaning "that is")

etc. (*Et cetera* –Latin for "and forth")

GRAB A GRAMMAR FACT

In an abbreviation, the last letter of the word and of the abbreviation may or may not be the same. Further, the pronunciation remains same whether we speak the full word or its abbreviated form unlike contractions.

- Mr – Mister (abbreviation)
- don't – do not (contraction)

GRAB A GRAMMAR FACT

In a contraction, the last letter of the word and of the contraction is the same. We DO NOT use a full stop with contractions. For instance,

I'll (I will)   she'd (she had)   it's (it has)

they've (they have)   we're (we are)   who'd (who would)

Understanding

We DO NOT use a full stop with abbreviations formed from the first capital letters.

Examples

BBC (British Broadcasting Corporation)

WWF (World Wildlife Fund)

MA (Master of Arts)

Remember!

Understanding

Whenever, there are three full stops in a row it indicates that the sentence is continued or something has been omitted. These are known as points or periods of ellipsis.

Example

Pandit Jawaharlal Nehru's most famous speech 'Tryst With Destiny' on the eve of India's Independence begins with, *"Long years ago we made a tryst with destiny, and now the time comes…"*

The three dots above show that we have quoted just a part of the speech.

A full stop is used after a single word that forms a sentence.

Examples

Go.

Wait.

Come.

Speak.

Understanding

A full stop is used after the initials of a person's name.

There you go!

Like, they call dad Mr M. Taylor.

Examples

E.M. Abbott – Edwin Milton Abbott

G.K. Chesterton – Gilbert Keith Chesterton

J.F. Kennedy – John Fitzgerald Kennedy

J.M. Fangio – Juan Manuel Fangio

PRACTICE

A. **Rewrite the following using capital letters and full stops wherever applicable.**

mrs daniel makes brilliant omelettes this is how she makes them take two eggs, a little butter, grated cheese and one finely chopped onion  first, take an egg beater and beat the eggs then melt the butter in a small frying pan and add chopped onions to the butter stir the onions pour the beaten egg mixture into the pan when it is nearly solid, turn it once and sprinkle the grated cheese on it fold the omelette into a semicircle and let the cheese melt for a few seconds serve hot

....

....

....

....

....

....

....

....

....

....

....

....

Follow the instructions.

Make two sentences, each
ending with a full stop.

....

....

Write two abbreviated words,
ending with full stops.

....

Give three contractions.

....

Give three abbreviations which
don't end with full stops.

....

Quote a part of a famous speech.
End it with ellipsis.

....

....

....

....

Write the initials of three people using full stops.

....

Understanding

A comma is used to organize thoughts into logical groups. It indicates a much shorter pause than a full stop. It separates the different parts of a sentence or names in a list.

A comma is used to separate a series of nouns.

Examples

1. My mother bought peas, tomatoes, carrots and potatoes from the food mart.
2. Our tour of Europe will take us to France, Germany, Italy and Netherlands.

GRAB A GRAMMAR FACT

- Always make sure that you use 'and' to separate the last two items in your list.
- Make sure that you don't use a comma before the word 'and' at the end of your list.

Understanding

A comma is used to separate a series of adjectives.

Examples

1. This tiny book has stories that are funny, inspirational, touching and thought-provoking.
2. My mother is an intelligent, confident, witty and a charming lady.

A comma is used to separate a series of verbs.

Examples

1. John ran, hopped, skipped and jumped on the sandpit.
2. Reading, listening to music, gardening and painting are some common hobbies people have.

A comma is used to enclose insertions or comments.

Example

The Vatican City, headquarters of the Roman Catholic Church, is the world's smallest country.

A comma is used where there is a little pause.

Examples

1. He was in the study room, preparing a presentation on the laptop.
2. I like bright colours, for instance, red, blue and orange.

Understanding

A comma is put after the words 'yes' and 'no' when they appear at the beginning of a sentence.

Examples

1. Yes, pack me five of those pastries.
2. No, I am too busy and cannot talk right now.
3. Yes, the boys have won the trophy.

Understanding

A comma is used to separate word pairs in a sentence.

Example

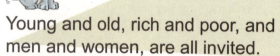

Young and old, rich and poor, and men and women, are all invited.

GRAB A GRAMMAR FACT

Between sentences, the most common mark of punctuation is the period; within sentences, the most common mark is the comma.

Understanding

We use commas with numbers.

That makes reading numbers easier.

Examples

1. Use a comma between the day of the month and the year.
   December 21, 1970 and July 20, 1969.
2. Use commas to show thousands, million and so on.
   1,000; 10,000; 100,000; 1,000,000

PRACTICE

A. **Insert commas where they are missing and rewrite the following sentences.**

1. My best friend lives at 23 Berlington Road Ohio.

   _____

2. I'm feeling fine thank you.

   _____

3. The names of my classmates are Rosy Peter John and Betsy.

   _____

4. Come along students. Yes you too Yunus.

   _____

5. Mom packed sandwiches juices wafers and pastries for the picnic.

   _____

6. Yes I am aware of the flight delay.

B. **Insert commas in the passage given below. (Hint: Commas are missing at 6 places.) Use red pencil colour.**

I went to my favourite ice cream parlour with my friends John Lisa Ted Nancy and Ben. The flavours of the day were chocolate fudge vanilla with peaches strawberry crush and coconut delight. I ordered strawberry crush ice cream with candy sprinkles walnuts and chocolate sauce on the top. It tasted yum!

Look at the pictures and list the characters/things you can see to complete each sentence. Make use of commas.

1.

.... are some famous fairy-tale characters.

2.

.... are some popular animated characters.

3.

.... are all means of transport that carry people and goods.

4.

.... are means of communication that help us to stay in touch with friends and relatives.

5.

.... are food items we get from animals.

Colon

Understanding

▲ **A colon is used to introduce a list.** ▼

Examples

1. For this experiment you will need: a beaker, a test tube, a measuring cyclinder and a teaspoon of salt.
2. Richard needs the following stationery items: pens, paper, pencils, highlighters and erasers.

Understanding

A colon is used after the subject in a formal letter.

Examples

1. Subject: Application for leave
2. Subject: Ordering goods

Subject: Resignation

Understanding

We use a colon between the hour and the minutes when we use numbers to express time.

Examples

1. 10:15 a.m.   2. 2:40 p.m.

Understanding

A colon is used to introduce a long or short direct quotation.

Examples

1. The aerobic teacher told the children: You need to wear proper clothes for your aerobic classes. Do not try any new exercise unless you are sure of the proper way.

2. Aesop said: "United we stand, divided we fall."

Understanding

We use a colon to separate two contrasting sentences/ideas.

Examples

1. Man proposes: God disposes.

2. One small step for man: one giant leap for mankind.

Understanding

A colon is used before examples.

Examples

1. These are some herbivorous animals: cow, goat, horse and zebra.

2. Here are some citrus fruits: orange, grapes, lemon and peach.

PRACTICE

A. **Using a red pencil colour insert colons at appropriate places.**

1. My father always says "If you help others, God will help you."

2. For this recipe, you will need a big onion (chopped), 50 grams of grated cheese, a tablespoon of butter and two eggs.

3. The water evaporated it turned into water vapour.

4. Two substances that can be dissolved in liquids sugar and salt.

5. These are the toppings I like on my pizza chopped onions, olives and extra cheese.

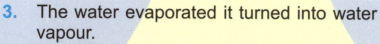
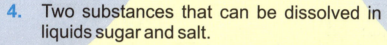
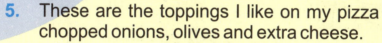

B. **Complete each sentence by adding a list of items after the colon.**

1. After dinner, we all had our favourite ice creams:

....

2. Nancy has to pack many things in her school bag:

....

3. John showed us the list of things to be carried to the school camp:

....

4. The following will be your schedule for the day:

....

5. Please ensure the delivery of the following goods:

....

Understanding

We use an exclamation mark after a strong interjection.

Examples

Understanding

We use exclamation mark after strong imperative sentences which mark certain direct commands.

Examples

An exclamation mark is used after exclamatory sentences.

Examples

What a lovely day!

This is a cool hat!

Understanding

An exclamation mark often accompanies sounds in a sentence.

Examples

1. In the zoo, the bear went "Grr!" as we looked on.
2. "Thud!" came the sound as she slipped in the bathroom.

Woof! Woof!

Tring! Tring!

PRACTICE

A. **Rewrite the paragraph by replacing full stops with exclamation marks wherever needed.**

"Did you see the new movie, Alien Attack?" asked Robert. "Ah, that movie. I saw it last evening with my sister Jennie," replied Peter. "It was great."

"O, my God. You call that a great movie?" Robert exclaimed. "I felt the aliens were looking too funny. What a waste of time."

Peter said, "Maybe you didn't like it, but I found the movie great. What fun we had."

....
....
....
....
....
....
....

B. **Make sentences using the following words. Put exclamation marks at appropriate places.**

Wow : ....
Hello : ....
Help : ....
Alas : ....
Ouch : ....

Understanding

A question mark is needed after a direct question. The question can be a short word or a whole sentence.

Examples

"Is he coming?"

"What? This is simply unbelievable."

"How much is this doll for?"

Can you guess who will win the race?

GRAB A GRAMMAR FACT

A full stop, a question mark and an exclamation mark are all used to:

1. end a sentence, and
2. mark the end of a complete thought.

PRACTICE

A. **Frame questions for the given answers and put question marks.**

1. Yes, this is a magic pen.

   ....

2. My dad is travelling to Beijing tonight.

   ....

3. No, the flowers in the vase are not real.

   ....

4. Yes, this umbrella is mine.

   ....

5. I love to play basketball.

   ....

B. **Write a letter to your grandma. Think of five things you would like to ask her. Jot them down in the letter.**

....

....

....

....

....

....

....

....

....

....

Understanding

A semicolon represents a pause greater than a comma.

We use a semicolon to separate the independent clauses of a compound sentence. Such clauses are NOT joined by a coordinating conjunction (and, but, or, nor, for, so, yet).

Examples

1. The fridge is empty; there is nothing in it.
2. I practice karate every day; my test is on Sunday.
3. The king was a wise, kind-hearted man; he was well respected.
4. People are usually willing to give advice; they are much less inclined to take it.

GRAB A GRAMMAR FACT

In separating the two clauses of a compound sentence, the semicolon is slightly stronger than a comma, but weaker than a period. Remember that the clause before the semicolon and the clause after the semicolon should be complete on their own; we should be able to replace the semicolon with a period and get two grammatically correct and complete sentences.

Semicolons are used in a series of three or more items when commas have already been used within the items.

Example

Appearing on tonight's show are Tweety, the yellow canary; Magic, the talking frog; and Barbie, the hip doll.

Understanding

We use a semicolon between two independent clauses which are joined by a conjunctive adverb (however, nevertheless, furthermore, then, therefore, moreover, etc.).

Examples

She works all day in a bank; furthermore, she takes music classes in the evenings.

John is an Australian; however, he lives in the United States.

You should get the car brakes fixed; otherwise, you might end up having an accident.

Hundreds of people use the metro to travel from one corner of the city to another; therefore, it is a hard task to keep it clean.

PRACTICE

1. I have lost my luggage and I don't know what to do.

    ....

2. My mother is a teacher and she is an author too.

    ....

3. Don't force your child to eat but be patient with her.

    ....

4. Take time to decide and you can call me next week.

    ....

5. I was feeling really sick in the morning but I am feeling better now.

    ....

B. **Use a colon or a semicolon to complete each sentence.**

1. I bring everything I need to class every day ⬚ my pens, my books and my dictionary.

2. This is what I told Pamela ⬚ "Buy yourself a colour box, so that you don't have to borrow mine!"

3. I had pasta for lunch ⬚ Fred had a sizzler.

4. The USA has a very large land area ⬚ Canada has even larger.

5. There are two things about him that drive me crazy ⬚ his forgetfulness and his carelessness.

31

Understanding

An apostrophe is used to show possession.

Examples

1. This is Robinson's school bag.
2. Lucy's mother is a doctor.
3. Mike's cousin found grandma's umbrella in Mr Frank's car.

Understanding

An apostrophe is used to show contraction or omission of letters.

Examples

Would you like to visit Darcy's place?

Yes, I'd love to!

1. Don't say sorry, as she's the one to be blamed.
2. He'll never talk to you now.

Understanding

When we refer to the plural of letters and words, we use apostrophe.

Examples

90's and 80's; x's and z's.

- An apostrophe indicates joint possession when used with the last of two or more nouns in a series: Snowy and Brown's kennel.

- It indicates individual possession when used with each of two or more nouns in a series: Snowy's and Brown's kennel.

PRACTICE

A. **Insert apostrophe (') wherever needed.**

1. The barbers shop
2. Miss Rosys class
3. Boys hostel
4. Kim and Cromwells room
5. Teachers staffroom
6. Officers mess
7. Marthas purse
8. Peacocks feathers
9. Kangaroos pouch
10. Banks parking space

B. **Insert apostrophe (') at appropriate places.**

1. The roads closed.
2. Mums surely going to find out our lie.
3. Wed love to watch Harry Potter and the Order of the Phoenix.

4. Whos moved my bag and hat?
5. The chemists shop is at the end of the road.
6. Miss Lee was standing at the bakers shop.

7. Its been raining all day.
8. At the zoo, the children were most interested in seeing the lions den.

Hyphen and Dash

Hyphen

Understanding

A hyphen is used to join together the parts of compound words.

Examples

1. The passer-by admired the beautiful garden.
2. Diana was very excited to meet her great-grandparents.

Understanding

We use a hyphen to separate compound numbers.

Examples

1. Seventy-five
2. Forty-six

Seventy – five glorious years
HAPPY PLATINUM ANNIVERSARY

Understanding

When we write a fraction in words, we use a hyphen.

Examples

Two-third of our planet is covered with water!

1. Two-fourth
2. One-third

Dash

Understanding

A dash is used to tag bits into a sentence.

Examples

1. Meet me at three–don't be late.
2. My grandfather–who is seventy–plays football.

Understanding

A dash sets apart an explanatory part of a sentence from the other parts.

Examples

1. Foods rich in protein–meat, fish and eggs–should be eaten on a daily basis.
2. Beverages–tea and coffee–are not good for children.

Understanding

A dash sets off the name of an author or source, such as at the end of a quotation.

Example

Minds are like parachutes. They only function when they are open.
—*Sir James Dewar*

GRAB A GRAMMAR FACT

At times a bracket is used instead of a dash to give some extra information within a sentence.

The cupboard (which had been in my family for years) was damaged while being shifted.

PRACTICE

A. **Match the following.**

Group – I	Group – II
1. Roll-	the-box
2. Tongue-	fetched
3. Cast-	tied
4. Jack-in-	off
5. Far-	call

B. **Rewrite after putting hyphen/dash at appropriate places.**

1. The designer displayed some eyecatching designs.

   ....

2. We were made to eat rockhard cookies.

   ....

3. I don't like your laidback attitude.

   ....

4. Green vegetables spinach, cabbage, broccoli, asparagus are essential parts of a healthy diet.

   ....

5. I'll turn twentyone this month.

   ....

6. All four of them Matilda, Emily, Sharon and Tracy did well in college.

   ....

Understanding

> **Double quotation marks enclose quotations.**

Examples

1. "Early to bed and early to rise makes a man healthy, wealthy and wise."
2. "Too many cooks spoil the broth."

Understanding

> **It marks a direct speech.**

Examples

1. "Nobody will leave the class without my permission," the teacher said.
2. Lopez asked Franklin, "May I borrow your atlas for awhile?"

GRAB A GRAMMAR FACT

- Quotation marks are used at the beginning and end of a phrase to show that it is being written exactly as it was originally said or written.
- Commas and periods are always placed immediately before the closing quotation mark.

PRACTICE

Put quotation marks wherever needed and rewrite the sentences.

1. No, I only planted flowering plants, answered Ashley.

....

2. This valley, said dad, is more beautiful than any other.

....

3. I love extra cheese on my pizza, said Martha.

....

4. Help! shouted the drowning boy.

....

5. Tom said, That's the coat I like.

....

FOR YOUR GRAMMAR SCRAPBOOK

Using strips of construction paper make a punctuation rainbow and paste it in your Grammar Scrapbook. For each punctuation mark, use a different coloured strip. You can use colours of your choice. Paste cut outs of each mark on its strip. Do you know that the rainbow in the sky is made up of seven colours—Violet, Indigo, Blue, Green, Yellow, Orange and Red (VIBGYOR)?

ANSWERS

PAGE 7

A. Indian, European, French, New Yorker, Chinese, Malaysian

B. (T)oday, me and my friend (T)ed drove to the (M)anchester (C)lub. (T)he pine trees that lined up along the main road looked beautiful! (W)e passed through the (R)iver (B)ridge. (T)hen we drove across the (T)om (S)quare (P)alace. (T)he guards outside the (P)alace did not let us in.

PAGE 14

A. Mrs Daniel makes brilliant omelettes. This is how she makes them. Take two eggs, a little butter, grated cheese and one finely chopped onion. First, take an egg beater and beat the eggs. Then melt the butter in a small frying pan and add chopped onions to the butter. Stir the onions. Pour the beaten egg mixture into the pan. When it is nearly solid, turn it once and sprinkle the grated cheese on it. Fold the omelette into a semicircle and let the cheese melt for a few seconds. Serve hot.

PAGES 19-20

A. 1. My best friend lives at 23 Berlington Road, Ohio.
   2. I'm feeling fine, thank you.
   3. The names of my classmates are Rosy, Peter, John and Betsy.
   4. Come along students. Yes, you too Yunus.
   5. Mom packed sandwiches, juices, wafers and pastries for the picnic.
   6. Yes, I am aware of the flight delay.

B. I went to my favourite ice cream parlour with my friends John, Lisa, Ted, Nancy and Ben. The flavours of the day were chocolate fudge, vanilla with peaches, strawberry crush and coconut delight. I ordered strawberry crush ice cream with candy sprinkles, walnuts and chocolate sauce on the top. It tasted yum!

C. 1. Little Red Riding Hood, Gingerbread Man, Pied Piper and Pinocchio
   2. Richie Rich, Snoopy, Bugs Bunny and Popeye
   3. Airplane, helicopter, ship and train
   4. Telephone, letters and e-mail
   5. Eggs, meat, honey and milk

PAGE 23

A. 1. My father always says: "If you help others, God will help you."
   2. For this recipe, you will need: a big onion (chopped), 50 grams of grated cheese, a tablespoon of butter and two eggs.
   3. The water evaporated: it turned into water vapour.
   4. Two substances that can be dissolved in liquids: sugar and salt.
   5. These are the toppings I like on my pizza: chopped onions, olives and extra cheese.

PAGE 26

A. "Did you see the new movie, Alien Attack?" asked Robert. "Ah, that movie! I saw it last evening with my sister Jennie," replied Peter. "It was great!"

"O, my God! You call that a great movie?" Robert exclaimed. "I felt the aliens were looking too funny. What a waste of time!"

Peter said, "Maybe you didn't like it,

but I found the movie great. What fun we had!"

PAGE 28
A. 1. Is this a magic pen?
   2. Where is your dad travelling tonight?
   3. Are the flowers in the vase real?
   4. Is this umbrella yours?
   5. Which game do you love to play?

PAGE 31
A. 1. I have lost my luggage; I don't know what to do.
   2. My mother is a teacher; she is an author too.
   3. Don't force your child to eat; be patient with her.
   4. Take time to decide; you can call me next week.
   5. I was feeling really sick in the morning; I am feeling better now.
B. 1. I bring everything I need to class every day [:] my pens, my books and my dictionary.
   2. This is what I told Pamela [:] "Buy yourself a colour box, so that you don't have to borrow mine!"
   3. I had pasta for lunch [;] Fred had a sizzler.
   4. The USA has a very large land area [;] Canada has even larger.
   5. There are two things about him that drive me crazy [:] his forgetfulness and his carelessness.

PAGE 33
A. 1. The barber's shop
   2. Miss Rosy's class
   3. Boys' hostel
   4. Kim and Cromwell's room
   5. Teachers' staffroom
   6. Officers' mess
   7. Martha's purse
   8. Peacock's feathers
   9. Kangaroo's pouch
   10. Bank's parking space
B. 1. The road's closed.
   2. Mum's surely going to find out our lie.
   3. We'd love to watch Harry Potter and the Order of the Phoenix.
   4. Who's moved my bag and hat?
   5. The chemist's shop is at the end of the road.
   6. Miss Lee was standing at the baker's shop.
   7. It's been raining all day.
   8. At the zoo, the children were most interested in seeing the lion's den.

PAGE 36
A. 1. Roll-call
   2. Tongue-tied
   3. Cast-off
   4. Jack-in-the-box
   5. Far-fetched
B. 1. The designer displayed some eye-catching designs.
   2. We were made to eat rock-hard cookies.
   3. I don't like your laid-back attitude.
   4. Green vegetables–spinach, cabbage, broccoli, asparagus–are essential parts of a healthy diet.
   5. I'll turn twenty-one this month.
   6. All four of them–Matilda, Emily, Sharon and Tracy–did well in college.

PAGE 38
1. "No, I only planted flowering plants," answered Ashley.
2. "This valley," said dad, "is more beautiful than any other."
3. "I love extra cheese on my pizza," said Martha.
4. "Help!" shouted the drowning boy.
5. Tom said, "That's the coat I like."